Does the Sky go on Forever?

poems and stories

TO: Jennifer & Ben

Best wishes!

— Mark Mc---

Does the Sky go on Forever?

poems and stories

Matt McConnell

MILL CITY PRESS

Minneapolis

Mill City Press, Inc.
212 3rd Avenue North, Suite 290
Minneapolis, MN 55401
612.455.2294
www.millcitypublishing.com

ISBN - 978-1-936107-40-7
ISBN - 1-936107-40-6
LCCN - 2009940377

Cover Design and Typeset by Kristeen Wegner

Printed in the United States of America

This book is dedicated to my family and friends with special thanks
to my wife, Betty, for her artistic and psychological support.
Also, thanks to my step-granddaughter, Emily, for her technical skills,
and to my daughter, Christina, and son, Ben,
for their advice and suggestions.

CONTENTS

Poems about People

Poems about Places and Times

Poems from other Voices

Poems about States of Mind

Stories

A Few Trifles

ANCHISES

Carried from the burning city of Troy
On the shoulders of his son, Aeneas,
Anchises reflects on the uncertainty
And brief duration of human glory.

He glances down at Ascanius, his grandson,
Trudging by his father's side
Toward an uncertain and perilous future.

Pious Aeneas, chosen by the gods or Fate
To found a new and greater empire
Than even that of Troy - one that in the irony
Of history will eventually conquer
The conquerers of Ilium.

But Anchises will never see that -
Will die in Sicily, then be visited
In the Underworld by his famous son.

Anchises was once a famous man, or youth,
For a brief moment, beloved by Aphrodite,
By the goddess of love herself, who bore
Their child, Aeneas, who now bears
His aged and ailing parent,
Who, bereft of strength and youth and beauty,
Clings to the fruit of his divine union.
And where is Aphrodite now?

　　The poem is an illustration of the ancient Roman saying, "Sic transit Gloria mundi" (so passes the glory of the world). Aphrodite, the goddess of love, fell in love with the youthful Anchises. Their offspring, Aeneas, is destined by the gods to found a new empire, that of Rome, which will eventually conquer the Greeks who had destroyed Troy (Ilium). Lost in all this turmoil is the fact that Aphrodite is long gone. For her, seemingly, it was "just one of those things."

TO FATHER WILL BRANDL

It's not just that we were friends
For twenty years;
Will went on and became a priest,
I "dropped out," as the saying goes.

It's not just that we stayed friends
For so long;
He married us, Rita and me.
We really married each other, of course,
But Will said the words, made it official.

And then he died, not yet forty
Of a brain tumor. Uneasy death.
Such a waste in human terms.
In movies, people die so beautifully.

It's not just all those things,
But that he is gone, and I am here.
It struck me so today.
Requiescas, Will, in pace.

ARNIE ON THE 18th

The long TV shot of Arnie
Trudging up the 18th fairway
For the last time at the Master's -
The huge gallery wildly cheering
The King and his Army.

Four times Arnie triumphed at Augusta;
Now, much older, slightly bowed,
With no chance of victory,
Now, in seeming contradiction
More victorious than ever in his fiftieth stroll
Up the 18th fairway at the Master's.

The Master himself in a red shirt,
Giving the thumb's up,
Carrying his doffed white cap,
Squinting into the sunlight.

How sweet the moment, the adulation -
How bittersweet this last march
Up the 18th fairway of the Master's
In Augusta, Georgia, Two thousand and four.

GALILEO

When Galileo first observed the moons of Jupiter
Through his optick tube,
He out-trod Columbus - star-sailed;
Opened up the heavens, and cracked
The old world-view.

The Nobel followed, right? Ticker-tape?
The Tonight Show? Film rights? A book deal?
Not quite.
Warnings, threats of torture, trials.

Why always these threats
From petty, jealous men;
Men concerned only
With their own uncertain glory?
But that's another story.

Matt McConnell

MISS MAPES

I first met Miss Mapes -
The late thirties - School District 117,
Me about seven, she hardly twenty,
A country school marm,
Always after me to read.
"Do you like to read, Matt?"
What I really liked were radio serials like
"Captain Midnight and the Secret Squadron!"
But Miss Mapes, who later married my oldest brother
Was insistent - "Read! Read!
You'll thank me some day."

We are both long retired now,
And Miss Mapes is ninety, now,
An age unimaginable to me at seven,
And even perhaps to Miss Mapes at twenty.
Lifetimes of age and centuries of reading
Homer to Virgil,
Dante to Shakespeare,
Pope to Frost.

And now, (better late than never),
Time to repay the debt owed Miss Mapes
And all my other teachers,
Those dispensers of the priceless gift
Of knowledge, and simply say,
"Thank you, Miss Mapes."

NAPTIME

He hears me coming down the hall
And scampers into bed.
I peer around the corner:
All is calm,
He is asleep.
I walk away and hear a creak,
Then a scampering to the toy box -
A sparrow chattering follows.
I stomp upon the floor -
Scamper, creak, silence -
Creak, scamper, chatter.
So it goes for an hour or two
Til naptime is over, and the topsy-turvy
World of two-year-olds is spun again
At breakneck speed.

Matt McConnell

ON STARTING FIRES

Education may be compared
To a journey from here - to there.
The "here" is so well known:
Home, ancestors, dogs - the rituals
Of everyday life - alarm clocks,
Schedules, making friends, eating desserts,
The street outside, winter, summer.

The journey's "there" is yet to be,
Unfocused, uncertain, with different houses,
Different friends, shadowy streets, unguessed fears,
Vague hopes of what we know not what.

Education, a wise man once observed,
Is not a basket to be filled with facts,
But a fire to be lit.
On the journey from here to there
Ally sets forth, armed with the love of those
Left behind, a satchel full of books,
A whole slew of intellectual desires,
And a box full of matches -
Ready to start some fires!

QUIZ

Where do the loons go in wintertime,
My daughter asks.
South - I sagely reply - South.
Mexico probably, someplace where
There's a lot of water.
Maybe Arkansas or Paraguay -
You're guessing, Dad, she says.

Matt McConnell

TO THE MEMORY OF MARTHA S.

Tiny, brief pilgrim,
Who lingered here
Only a day -
Then spread wings,
And flew away.

HEDDA ON THE SIDEWALK

Passing Hedda Gabler on her way home
From the Guthrie - not Hedda
Herself but the actor who portrayed her,
I am brought face to face with a
Strange phenomenon - a conflict of realties:
The Hedda of the stage
Lives and talks and finally dies on stage,
While the actor who portrays her
Who pretends to die by self-inflicted
Gunshot wound, now walks
Briskly along the sidewalk to her apartment (I suppose)
At 4 p.m.of a grey September afternoon.
(Hedda hated September),
And who will return to the theater this evening
To act and talk, sneer at her husband, Tesman,
Ward off the jackal-like advances of Judge Brach,
And die again by her own hand, incapable
Of sustaining the courage to be, in a world
Grown harsh beyond endurance.

Hedda Gabler, tragic heroine of the famous play, HEDDA GABLER, by Henrik Ibsen.

Matt McConnell

SILENT MEETING

It was a long time before we met again,
At the theater, I with my brother,
You with a friend.
I saw you look intently at the stage,
On imitation of life, on showy rage
Of simulated grief.
Then our eyes met – no brief
Lightening flash betwixt us then,
Only a silent "hello friend."
And "shall we start again?"
Settled. And no one heard.
Amazing what can be said
Without a word.

TONY O.

When Tony Oliva was young,
He was a son-of-a-gun of a baseball player.
He could catch and hit and run
Like a deer,
And win batting titles year after year
Til his knees gave out,
And Tony's career was done.

SOCRATES

Fifty years he nagged them,
Questioning their priorities.
They endured the gadfly for a spell,
But no one likes such stinging.
So eventually they put him away.
Too bad for them.

One quest he was bound to fail -
Finding a wise man, a search dearer
To him than any grail.
(He never looked into a mirror).

HEROES

We prefer our heroes dead
For the most part - tidier that way
And more stirring:
The flag-draped coffin,
The service at the grave site,
Crackling rifles,
Taps - the sounds that tear the heart,
The neatly folded flag
Cradled in white dress gloves
Presented to the bereft wife or mother -
Dust to dust.

Otherwise, the long hospital ordeal,
Disfiguring burns, persistent nightmares,
Or the shell-shocked skulls that can endure
For years, decades even,
Languishing in run-down soldiers' homes.
Dolce et decorum est, etc.
As Horace once ruefully observed.
But not to die can be hard - hard -
More grievous, perhaps, than folded flags,
Crackling rifles, or the crystal sound of taps
Drifting across sun-drenched autumnal fields.

    Famous line from one of the odes of the Roman poet, Horace. The full quote is, "Dulce et decorum est pro patria mori." (It is sweet and proper to die for the Fatherland)

Matt McConnell

TO EMILY –
ON HER HIGH SCHOOL GRADUATION

In the Divine Comedy, Dante
Is guided through the Inferno
And the Purgatory by Virgil,
A pagan who cannot enter Paradise.
So Virgil, the faithful protector
Simply vanishes, no longer needed,
His mission done.
We can imagine his anguish
And sense of loss, but also perhaps relief,
Also perhaps happiness
Knowing he had finished his work
And that love endures beyond separation.

Now Emily moves on.
Life is all endings and beginnings,
All flux and change,
Tides rising and ebbing -
Love is the constant,
And she must know for certain
That the love of those left behind
Won't change, as Dante, even in Paradise
Must have recalled Virgil's devotion.

JOURNEY

In the small back bedroom of my in-laws' house
In Hustler, Wisconsin,
Hangs a photograph of Harland Hanson.
Bespectacled, wearing the uniform and cap
Of World War II,
He smiles gently at the camera.
In 1945, aged 23,
Harland died in Holland, in a POW camp,
His spirit broken, glasses smashed.

I stare at Harland's face, at a man
I never knew - my wife's uncle - and wonder
What his death matters,
Just one of how many victims of that time?
No victory parades for him -
No wife or child -
No life's work -
Like Keats, who died in Rome by the Spanish steps,
Harland is forever young.

After the war, he was carried back
And laid to rest, here in Wisconsin ground.
To Harland, it made no difference:
To the dead, earth is earth -
Dust is dust.

John Keats, famous English poet, was only twenty-six when he died.

Poems about
Places and Times

NORTH FROM ATLANTA

In north Georgia, a hundred miles
Up from Atlanta, somewhere around Blairsville,
The lake curlicues around green hills.
In the distance, range after range
Of low mountains melt into gauze.
We pontoon the greenish water,
Gorging ourselves on sandwiches and grapes.
Always underfoot,
The dogs sprawl every which way.

As the reddish sky fades into purple and rose,
It's silly word games and talk-talk-talk
Late into the night
On subjects great and small.

At early morning light,
We stand on the deck,
Drink coffee,
And gaze at the mist-shrouded water
Cool as a dream,
Which will soon give way to summer's heat.
What day of the week is it? We ask blankly.

Matt McConnell

NOVEMBER WALK

At 7:00 p.m., the full moon
Sits in Eastern Splendor.
Down the street, dry leaves
Scurry along the curbing
Toward some leafy rendezvous.
Pale jet contrails
Stretch across the sky,
One gauzing o'er the moon.
A few Christmas lights
Are strung already
Like nervous early comers.
Soon we turn home.
No traffic.
Up the street, a lorn dog
Bays at the peerless sky.

PEARL HARBOR DAY - 1991

You see them on TV - these (now) old men
Telling how it was back then - in '41,
Of the sudden terror and disbelief
As the torpedo bombers swept in, low over the water,
Of the smell of burning flesh and oil,
Of friends lost, bodies shattered,
As the great ships rolled sideways and sank.

Fifty years later, the greying veterans
Speak of these things, and the tears come
And the voices break - even after fifty years.
Some things we are never healed of.

In 1991, the 50th anniversary of the Pearl Harbor attack, a television show interviewed some of the survivors of that event.

Matt McConnell

DYING VILLAGE

Lost in the sloping hills and farmlands
Of North Dakota, lies a tiny hamlet
With gravel streets, about a dozen houses,
One rusty-looking store, a shell-shed,
And a rectangular brick building.
Across the front, near the top,
In neat letters is the legend,
FARMERS   TATE BANK.
A sign hangs at right angles
Just below those letters, proclaiming
"Joe's Groceries - Lockers."
The door is bolted and the two windows
To the right of the door
Are boarded up.

ALBUQUERQUE

Albuquerque, Albuquerque,
Just a hint of something murky.
Is your interest a little quirky?
You may find it in Albuquerque.

Albuquerque, Albuquerque,
If your nerves are herky-jerky
And would like to feel more perky,
Just stop in at Albuquerque.

Albuquerque, Albuquerque,
If you like to chew beef jerky,
And love to hunt the wild turkey,
Take a trip to Albuquerque.

Matt McConnell

COME SEPTEMBER (TO N AND J)

Come September, the school year starts anew,
Autumn flowers bloom,
The slightly smoky air
Tastes different than in April.
Summer is passing, and winter -
Only a faint foreboding.

Come September, no better time
To join hands, exchange the vows,
And say to one and all -
Springtime is joyous,
Summer - glorious -
But, ah, September!
When love, like the aster blossoms,
Matures, and looks contentedly
At all things, then and now.

COSMOS

It all started, the physicists tell us,
With a big bang – a cosmic firecracker.
God said, "let there be light!"
And the whole shebang went off.
Talk about your Roman candles!

The universe began in those first
Micro seconds, and in that expansion
From unity to diversity
We were there – or here – already,
In a way.
Stars would have to live
And die first, true; stellar cookouts;
(We are such stuff as stars are made of).
And our frail bodies mirror
The complexity of the vast world
That stretches to the quasars and beyond.

Stars and planets; classical, romantic;
Atoms and elephants; past and future;
Mystery and knowledge; light and dark;
Blue and red shifts; meson and quark;
Galaxies and motes; the one and the many;
Life and death; pain and bliss.
Did God foresee all this?
Or was he just playing with fire
And the cosmic egg blew up,
Unexpectedly?
No, that can't be right,
For God distinctly said,
"Let there be light."

Matt McConnell

THE NAME FOR RAIN IS MIST

The name for rain is mist
Drifting o'er the clovered field,
Glistening the new fall plowing,
Beading on the barbed fence,
Then infiltrating the woods,
Each branch and twig,
The dark piled leaves,
Stifling all noise, even the sulky crow
To the softest murmurs,
Turning all nature into damp twilight.

WINTER TREES

Winter trees are minimalists.
Bare trunks and branches show their skeletal shapes.
Long gone the light greens of spring,
Departed, mid-July's darker hues,
Absent, the garish tints of autumn.
Winter shows the essence of naked wood -
Except for the oaks, those contrarians
Who still cling to their rusty foliage
Until in mid-April, new generations of buds
Consign them, sans regret
To the leaf-strewn forest floor.

Matt McConnell

UP NORTH AT THE LAKE

Up north at the lake
A summer evening storm -
Wind lashing the dark water,
White caps crashing against the dock,
Pine cones scuttle across the deck,
While safely inside, we watch the rain
Spatter against window panes.

Next morning, gentler water, a clean sky.
Gulls bobble on the waves like corks -
In the distance, sailboats lean into the breeze -
Two fishing boats, unmoving as a still life
Wait patiently for the elusive prey.

In winter, the lake, like a vast snowy cornfield
Stretches flatly into the distance.
Only a faint memory now
Of water skiing and eerie loon.
Only ice-clad silence now,
And snow sifting down through red pine tops.
Time moves slowly here,
Up north, at the lake.

NURSING HOME

The staff is mostly young,
Relentlessly cheerful:
"How are we today, Alice?"
"Dying."
(Alice is such a card!)

It's true, though.
Alice waits for death,
Clings to life,
Wheelchair-ridden
In this pleasant storage house.

In ancient times,
When the tribe moved on
The old, the infirm
Of necessity, were left behind.
Much the same way now.
Going hence is harder
Than coming hither.
And more lonely.

Matt McConnell

MIGRATION

In the wintry distance the geese,
Black and white, sail in on invisible currents
Towards the cornfield, wingtips bent down,
Long necks arching upwards –
Miniature supersonic transports.

Sometimes, on early February afternoons,
They lift off, back to the lake,
Thousands at once, darkening the sky,
Cackling noisily about Schopenhauer,
The high price of corn, and that soon
The irresistible genetic code
Will drive them north to Canada.

"OH, CANADA!"

They intone, as they fall
Toward the dark water.

When Spring comes, all will depart for the North –
All but the broken-winged.

Arthur Schopenhauer, 1788-1860, German philosopher.
How the geese came to know anything about him, I have no idea.

JAMESTOWN

I am sitting on the bed
In a small hotel room
In Jamestown, North Dakota.
It is late August,
Chilly, grey, on a Sunday afternoon.
Rain is tum-tumming on the low slanted roof.
The wheat is only fifty percent harvested,
And freezing nights will soon be here
In North Dakota. I will be here
Only a week longer, but endless
Green sloping hills, stubble fields,
And frusty little towns with dusty gravel
Streets will stay to endure
The wind chill of November.

Three poems recalling
a trip to London

THE MUSEUM GOER'S LAMENT

I was late at the Tate
For meeting my wife.
She had said, "be there at two!"
But it wasn't til three,
After risking my life
In the traffic - no clue
Where she would be
For our date at the Tate.

"Meet me," she'd ordered
"In the room filled with Turners."
But to my chagrin,
Around every corner and down endless hallways
There were rooms after rooms filled with Turners,
Of his paintings early and middle and late
At the Tate.

So I pondered my fate
As I wandered about
Greatly fearful that wrath
From my disgruntled mate
Would descend on my pate
When I met her at last,
Because I was late at the Tate.

Matt McConnell

WAY OUT

In London Town
You will never get lost
If you follow this simple advice:
"Go straight on
To the end of the street
Then bend left, then two rights,
Then straight on
Til you see the sign – **WAY OUT**

A COLLECT FOR THE MONKS

Long, long ago
Before Disraeli, or the Third George -
Go further back, before Charles Two,
Elizabeth One or Henry the Seventh,
Clear to Chaucer's boyhood.
In 1348, the black slab
On the Abbey floor declares
That twenty-six monks of Westminster
Perished of the Black Death.
No need to collect their scattered bones. All here.
Worn is the slab under which they lie,
By footsteps through the days
And weeks, months and years of centuries.
Through different reigns, brutal wars,
New worlds discovered, into a new millenium,
And through all this stretch of time, from then til now
The twenty-six monks have lain here patiently
Beneath the black slab in Westminster Abbey.
In Pace, Requiescant.

Collect (emphasis on first syllable) a brief prayer, read before the epistle, and that varies from day to day. No longer used now generally in religious services.

Matt McConnell

JANUARY FLIGHT

It is mid January, 5:30 p.m. -
A mild winter's early eve.
The sky is not yet black
And a faint pink still tints
The lighter West.

I stand in Barlow's parking lot
Clutching my bag of groceries - gaping.

The geese approach in waves
Still two miles off,
A hundred or more to a formation
Which stretches a quarter mile wide,
Bow-shaped.

The half moon, trailed by Jupiter
Sits high, just left of south.

The geese are nearer now, their lines
Undulating, breaking, reforming.
Now they are overhead, soaring
At 50 miles an hour,
(Well above the posted limit).
They sweep across the moon
And vanish into darker East.

TIME

In the world of the cosmologists,
Time is an ancient thing.
Only God, perhaps, is patient enough
To outwait its geologic extent,
Those eons that stretch
From eternal to eternal,
Measured in earth years,
Reaching back beyond
The forming of our sun,
And forward to a burned-out star,
A frozen earth.
Fragility is ours.

Matt McConnell

YORKTOWN

Mortally stricken off Midway
With all her crewmen gone,
The aircraft carrier Yorktown,
Seeking a resting place,
Falls three miles down,
Smashes into the ocean floor
Her armor rattling, the guns all silent now.

In Homer's *ILIAD*, the stricken warrior,
Sternum pierced by the spear thrust
And darkness rushing past his eyes,
Crashes to earth,
Seeking a resting place,
Battle harness rattling in the dust
His weapons silent now, all useless.

The Yorktown lies silent now,
Lost in the lightless deeps of the wine-dark sea.

Poems from Other Voices

MEMORIAL DAY

They are leaving just now.
My daughter bends down,
Whispers, "love you – Mother – love you."
Her children fretful, anxious to go
On this sunlit day.
Her husband, Nick, waves a self-conscious farewell.
 "Farewell," I whisper back.
She comes several times a year.
It's hard, living so far away.
My other daughter who lives nearby,
Comes not at all, not even on Memorial Day.
I sigh. Too late now
To go back, to undo what has been done,
Or left undone, untended.

It is late afternoon already.
Time passes swiftly here, so swiftly,
And the tall monument nearby, with the angel
Perched atop, already casts its long shadow
Across half the cemetery.
My husband, John, who lies beside me here,
And who seldom speaks,
Says, "never mind, Nell. Never mind it.
Go to sleep."

THE GIRL

She created quite a stir
In the upscale bar.
Well-dressed men, well up
The ladder of success, made casual
Obscene comments, sotto voce,
Reclining on her cantilevered bosom.
Leg men, with practiced eyes,
Drifted over taut calves.
Her back was naked to the waist,
The face heavily clothed;
Pale-powder flesh – red lips;
She exuded Arabian nights,
An earthly Paradise, delights.

Lilies and roses,
Lilies and roses,
All bring posies to the girl.
Lilies are pale,
Roses are red,
Wine her and dine her
And take her to bed.

When Helen walked upon the wall
The elders in the courtyard
Followed her with craving eyes,
And she accepted their worship
With nonchalant and gracious understanding.

She sat at the bar,

Matt McConnell

Waiting for a certain person,
Sipping her Daiquiri.
She tossed her head
To clear the mist cast up
By the prow of Paris' ship.
A cloven-footed someone
Came from the mist
And whispered something indistinct.
She turned,
And gave him a withering look.

The Helen, is Helen of Troy – the most beautiful woman in the world. Her effect upon men was pretty much instantaneous. After abducting Helen, Paris, a son of the Trojan king, sailed with her to Troy.

A SATIRE

Written after a perusal of the Earl of Rochester's
"A Satire Against Mankind."

I had in mind, the other day,
To write "A Satire on Mankind."
Nothing personal you understand;
To be general, not specific.
After all, the aim of satire,
So I'm given to understand,
Is to lash the foolish things
That apply to all – but me.
So you see, a good beginning
Would be – hmm – it's hard, you know,
Where to start. Pride of place?
Love of money? Vainness of a
Sculptured face! Success with ladies?
Affectation? Swiftness in the dusty race
Of dog eat dog laissez-faire?

"I'm a self-made man, you know;
Don't say I can't keep the pace.
Pulled myself up by the bootstraps –"

Which is, I'm sure, a special grace
Since the law of gravitation
Must apply in every place.
Furthermore, in that position,
Since man is brittle as a vase,
Mustn't he then break his – well,

Matt McConnell

I had in mind, the other day
To write "A Satire on Mankind."
But then, you know, I'm much too humble
Gentle, kind, and debonair
To reveal the faults of others.
And after all, most people, really
Are pretty wonderful in fact –
Except for Judy, Dick and Jack.

DESPAIR

How far am I from despair today?
Well, on a scale of 1 to 10,
With 1 being absolute TV sitcom
Cheeriness, and 10 representing
The noose in the basement -
Probably about a 7.
Still handable, the mental health folks
Might say - no need to take away
My belt and shoestrings yet.

Matt McConnell

SOLDIER

I am only forty-seven years old
But I feel ancient – worn.
Let me introduce myself,
A retired soldier, named Jacob.
I served under Herod the King.
One day the order came –
Kill all the male children
Under two years old.
We thought briefly of mutiny,
But several who did were crucified.
We heard their long screams.
And so, we did our work.
How many? I can't remember now.
I have burned away most memories
Of that time – but not all.
Not all.
Even in the daylight hours,
I can still smell the blood,
Feel the blood.
Nighttimes are the worst.
I don't sleep much anymore –
And Herod the King is long since dead.

WISDOM IN THE A.M.

Ten to five already!
Kara out of the shower, doing her face.
In twelve minutes, she'll be gone
In her BMW, til Thursday,
On business, in Philly.

I dress fast, time's awasting,
Can't be late for the 7:00 a.m.
Prayer/Business meeting.
Quick sips (thank God for the pre-set coffee maker).
Quick kiss. "Will miss you!" She's gone.
Quick check: 159 emails on the laptop.

On the way now. Garage door folding up,
Start the SUV (so sweet!)
Back out fast. Wham! Hit the brakes!

She is resting by the curb in a long blue hooded cape,
Beautiful, an unmistakable sight -
Wisdom - sitting by my gate in the early morning light.
She smiled and beckoned me (so sweet!)
To sit down by her side,
But I didn't have time
Cause I had to get to the PARK 'N RIDE.

See Book of Wisdom 6:12-16: Whoever watches for her at dawn shall not be disappointed, for he shall find her sitting by his gate.

Matt McConnell

DEEP INSIDE PLATO'S CAVE

Deep inside Plato's cave,
Chained to the floor,
Staring straight ahead,
The shadowy figures dance before me,
Weave and twist, dissolve and merge.
They are all I've ever known
Since I first began to know.

Behind me, suddenly,
And in a whispered voice,
Someone I cannot see says urgently,
"This is not reality.
What you see now - only shadows.
Outside the cave the sun shines brightly -
The glowing color of flowers, the music of birds
Will pierce your heart - come with me!"

I cannot leave, I say.
The chain does not allow it,
And I fear the sun will blind me.
The color of flowers, the songs of birds,
Will break my heart.
Better here, in safety,
Lulled by these flickering flames.
The gentle grey prisoners, my silent companions,
Murmur their agreement.
The voice behind me sighs and is gone.

And once again the mute shadows
Dance and gyrate on the wall before me - here -
Deep inside Plato's cave.

In his long philosophical work, THE REPUBLIC, Plato, in the myth of the cave, pictures us as prisoners in a cave where we see only shadowy images of reality. To journey upward to the outer real world involves effort and risk. So most choose the easy way, stay in the cave and be content with shadows.

Matt McConnell

FLIGHT INTO EGYPT

I, Joseph, the carpenter,
Dreamed last night.
I dream sometimes, but almost always
By mid-morning, they are gone.
But this one - the young man
All in white, so dazzling it was
Painful to look at him.

You must leave, he said,
You must fly into Egypt
At dawn. The child
Is in grave danger from Herod the King.
He vanished. I woke,
My heart beating hard.
I was - angry, confused.
It is winter, I thought,
The nights cold, the baby colicky,
Fretting - his mother still frail
And in pain from childbirth.
My thoughts raged against Herod,
The king of a world so evil.
Men like Herod - when they die
What do they put on their grave markers?
"I slaughtered infants? Burnt whole villages?
Caused panic, smashed houses?
Showed no mercy?"
Had Herod been in my grasp that moment -

I felt Mary's hand touch my hand.

She was cloaked already -
The infant cradled in her arms.
"We must leave, Joseph," she said.
I stared at her dumbly for a moment,
Uncomprehending.
She smiled gently. "Now, Joseph.
We must leave now."
So I seated her and the infant,
Now sleeping, on the beast.
And as we passed through the doorway,
I turned its head southward,
As the last stars were fading
Into morning light.
South, towards Egypt.

CLARISSA

Well now, that's a hard question to answer.
I've known a lot of women in my day
And not a few of them were handsome.
Maybe not so hard though, after all.
After all, I'm getting on, and times past
Have a harder clarity than just last week.
I call to mind, when I was just about your age -
It was a golden summer that year,
The crops were good,
And if I remember rightly
The corn went sixty bushel.
Clarissa was her name, and to my amorous eyes
She was the loveliest thing
That ever walked the earth.
She had gold-brown hair and blue eyes
And a face and form that set all eyes aglow.
I saw her seldom, never spoke to her,
But worshipped at a distance, so to say.
Well, at the county fair that year, she was there
And I was there, but not together.
That was the only time I ever spoke to her.
Like a lovesick crazy fool I followed her around
The dusty fairgrounds, and then as if the hand
Of fate had interceded for me, someone
Bumped against her and she dropped her purse.
That was my chance, and believe me
I didn't let it pass. I sprang forward
And picked it out of the dust and gave it back to her.
Clarissa smiled at me and said

"Thank you, William." God in Heaven!
All I could do was turn beet-red and stammer
"You're welcome." That was the last time
I ever saw her for she soon went east
To some school and later married a wealthy man.
And I too have become a somewhat wealthy man
For what that's worth. But never in all these
Sixty years have I forgot Clarissa. The memory of her
Is still green and young and fair though
I am old and she walks on the earth no more.
All things change, grow old and die,
But to me Clarissa is still young and fair
With gold-brown hair and blue eyes
And a face and form that set my heart aglow.
The currents of time flow on without remorse,
And their erosion has wrought great change in me -
But not Clarissa. She is to me
An island in the river
That runs down to the sea.

Poems about States of Mind

PARTING AND MEETING

Far out from land
Aeneas glances back to shore;
Does he dimly see
The heaped-up pyre
And storm-tossed Dido
Plunging the blade into her breast?

The Fates that force him on,
Drive her to this blood-letting.

They will meet again in the dark world
So unlike Carthage -
The lethal wound unclotted,
Her heart still set against him,
Deaf to all his pleas
As she drifts back to her pale Sychaeus.

After fleeing the burning city of Troy, Aeneas lands in Carthage, whose queen is Dido, the widow of Sychaeus. Aeneas and Dido fall in love, but Fate eventually forces him to leave to found the Roman Empire. In despair, Dido kills herself. Later, visiting the Underworld, Aeneas sees Dido, who still hates him for his desertion of her.

Matt McConnell

TEMPUS FUGIT

My forty-third year, for example,
Which occurred sometime back,
I don't recall at all.
Like smoke rising from a mountain campfire,
The years drift up through tree tops,
Thin out and vanish.

ALIEN CORN

When the aliens come
They will, of course, be
"Technologically superior" to us;
Able to leap, in a single bound
Whole skies in single alien days;
Carry laser blasters, have sentient robots,
Be amused at our childish ways.

What of the world they come from?
Do alien butterflies,
In alien fields of corn,
Flutter there?
What do alien trees look like?
Alien sunsets? Alien bass?
Alien moons, casting criss-crossed shadows
On alien grass?

And do the aliens themselves, conical,
Quadruped or mandrake-shaped
Dream alien dreams, feel pain,
Write alien sonnets, make angel shapes,
In alien snow?

If they be too unlike us
How shall we ever know?

Matt McConnell

INSPIRATION

I wanted to write a poem today.
One should keep in practice, I suppose,
Lest the muse lose interest
And drift away.
What about? There's the rub.
No one's died recently (rules out elegy).
Love? Not in the mood.
How about something deep and obscure?
Yes!
Something on the human condition or
The absurdity of life - or something.
No!
Not on a warm day in early spring
When the first robin shatters and
Shoos away the last tatters of winter,
And shows under dark, piled leaves,
Soft as pillows, the first shoots,
And the faint green gauze
That clothes the river willows.

THE BUTTERFLY

Always I pursue you
As you flutter just out of reach.
Tireless, I consume my days, captive
To such a slender thing.

Slyly I ready my net,
Shyly you dance just out of reach;
Slowly I turn in the dance of love,
Deftly you elude my clumsy net.
Furious I curse the empty sky,
Curious you turn and cease to fly
And settle on a slender twig.

Cautious I approach and lowly speak,
Lovingly you gaze and brush my cheek.
Softly you say the words I seek,
"My love - my only one" -
Longingly I know you will not stay,
Silently you rise and drift away.

Matt McConnell

IF ONLY

If only Galileo had a laptop
As he circled up the Leaning Tower -
If only Shakespeare, a ballpoint pen
And a yellow legal pad -
Keats, a decent medical plan -
Socrates, the pension plan
He so justly argued for -
Swift, an anti-depressant,
Milton, a skilled optometrist,
Beethoven, a modern hearing aid -
How much richer the world might be,
Not that they didn't contribute mightily
As it was - but think if only
Queen Elizabeth, a painless dentist,
The Mona Lisa, a dental whitener --

FIN

Dante, in a sense, had it right after all.
His lower Hell, you may recall,
Is a place of ice, sleet, and freezing winds.

So, when the end came, God decided to do it
The Dante way: not with sodomish brimstone
That reduces all to a glimmer
Of ash, but with frost that pierces to the core.

He simply dimmed out the sun
Til there was nothing left but a sliver
Of light, and that's how it ended -
Not with a sweat, but a shiver.

Matt McConnell

DEFYING GRAVITY

In the early evening, from my balcony
Three hundred feet above the Mississippi
The jet crosses my line of vision.
Climbing to the east, defying gravity,
It struggles upwards,
Fleeing the earth, and soon may
For all I know in my unscientific ignorance
Pull free from earth itself,
Sweep past the moon,
Escape the gravitation of the sun,
Head for outer space, into the galaxy -
Destination Andromada,
Or the Crab Nebula at least,
And put down at last in Detroit.

Andromada – a large, spiral galaxy, similar to our Milky Way galaxy. It is about 2.2 million light years from earth, so the possibility of a celestial collision is very small. In Greek mythology, Andromada is the wife of Perseus, who had rescued her from a sea monster.

Crab Nebula – the remnants of a super nova star, within the Milky Way galaxy that exploded in 1054 A.D. It can be seen only by telescope, and is one beautiful celestial sight.

ELEGY

But my heart betrays me,
O treacherous rebel that, unbidden,
Leaps in its place when your eyes meet mine.
I am helpless in your gaze.
I long to touch you – to embrace.
Embrace! (seductive word).

My mother said the only time
She ever saw my father weep
Was once, during the Depression
He thought he would lose the farm.
He was a farmer, first and last.
To lose his land
Would have been like a death to him.

But fortune ever changes, she gives with one hand,
Takes with another – nothing is sure.
We think we are secure. We build our
Wall of sand upon the beach,
Safe behind our battlements.
Then looking seaward, we espy
In the distance, a wall of water
Fifty feet in height, driving shoreward,
Its roar increasing, blotting out the sky.

Paralyzed, we crouch behind our wall of sand -
And now the wave is on us.
Upward in terror we look – a cruel force
Of green foam crashes down

And the farm is gone,
And gone is my beloved – ah ha you say –
Now we get to it, at last; all this stuff
Just a lament for a lost love!
Yes, I answer – simply that.
Only a lament. An elegy of sorts.

THE GATE

She has gone to that land beyond our land.
She has passed through the gate
That closed immediately behind.
I try to peer beyond the grate
But cannot see.

What celestial geography does she now explore?
Has she passed through other gates,
Other rooms and doors that close behind?

Life is a journey, they say.
Is death a journey, too?
She has gone to that land beyond our land.
(And does not return.)

Matt McConnell

PLANETS

Jupiter rises in the east
Pursued by Mars.
Lordly, majestic, they careen
Across the night sky.

But why?

Low in the west, silent, serene,
Venus shines dazzling.
All in vain. They cannot catch her,
Enchanting as the voice of the lute.

No matter.

What matters is the pursuit
Of Venus, vision of light,
Loveliest of all starry beams
As she plunges each night
Into the ocean streams.

OCTOBER SUN

The troubled mind boils
Like the sun, that great
Ball of gas that roils
In power unimaginable
To us.

The sun at midday
Blinds the eye that seeks
Its beauty.

But at midmorning
Of an early October day,
Returning from the hospital,
From the locked ward,
The landscape mist-shrouded,
The sun is but a pale disk
Shrunk to moon size,
Flitting through tree tops,
Giving scant light
And no warmth.

Matt McConnell

PRAYER

(Prayer composed after attending a production of
Arthur Miller's *The Crucible*).

From the faith of our forefathers,
O Lord, deliver us.

SENTRY

Like the sentry at his post
My dark seems endless.
Then your love's first ray
(Oh, longed-for sight)
In radiant ambers and gold
Dawns my night.

Why do you affect me so?
What subtle power dwells within those eyes?
Your glance, sunlike,
Blinds me with its noonday glow.

The twilight comes anon.
Hold me through your cloudless day
Lest Oedipus-like,
I stumble in the dark.

Matt McConnell

QUIET TIMES

In the quiet times, at evening,
Sitting alone, I think of you.
I stare out the window
At nothingness, and think of you.
Of you, and times past,
Of things that could not be.

Beloved, from time to time
In the quiet times, at evening,
Think of me.

VISIONS

Lady at the Guthrie with red painted toenails
At intermission, leaning on the balcony rail.
Slim, serious face, large round glasses, honey-brown hair -
Glancing at her sideways, my heart nearly fails,
Gold-strapped heels showing red painted toenails.

In my fancy, as director, I cast her as Helen -
Wait! Not so - her beauty is of a gentler kind,
Like Iphigenia, whose frail youthfulness
Is sacrificed at Aulis to gain the favoring wind.
I see her terrified, gagged, unable to rouse pity
As coarse hands hoist her high above the rail.
And Agamemnon, too dense to read the future,
Unthinking that Clytennestra, that fierce wife and mother
Would ever forgive this heinous crime.
He will return one day from Troy, triumphant,
Cassandra, with long black hair, casually in tow,
Only to die in the homecoming.
But now, seeing only his own needs,
Gives the fatal sign, and Iphigenia shudders
As the knife drives inward,
Spraying her blood on those murderers.

It is too harsh, I can watch no more.
As the bell sounds, I turn from the balcony
And my eye catches - what is that?
A vision - there! There! In the harbor -
Dozens, hundreds, a thousand swelling sails -
Lady at the Guthrie with blood spattered nails.

A complex and dysfunctional family. Agamemnon led the Greek forces in the war against Troy to recapture Helen who was married to his brother. In order to gain the favoring winds to sail from the port of Aulis, Agamemnon sacrifices his daughter, Iphigenia. When he returns home ten years later, a victor, his wife Clytemnestra, kills him in revenge. The rest of the poem is just made up. The Guthrie Theater is real.

WINDMILL

In her ninety-first year, my mother
Cannot speak, cannot raise her head or hand.
The Indignant Hours have beat her down,
Who at twenty-three, outpaced my father
And two hired hands as she raced,
Hair streaming behind,
A hundred yards to the windmill
To rescue Bitty Boy (her second son)
From the water tank.

Driving back from the nursing home
I pass shorts-clad high school girls
Running, practicing cross country,
Lithe legs gleaming in the sun,
Hair streaming behind
As they race toward that distant windmill.

Matt McConnell

SUNSET

Driving home on Highway 52,
In early December, the fantastic sunset
Plays out its drama for me.
(With no admission charge at all).

Never before in the whole history of the Cosmos
Nor in the future, will such a scene
In such exact detail of cloud and color
Or in such splendor, be reprised.

I stop awhile to gaze in wonder,
Cars whizzing by at 80 miles an hour,
Unconcerned that my existence is also unique, fleeting,
And as insubstantial as the flaming sky.

Stories

BREAKING OPEN THE PEANUTS

At seven years old, living on a farm was not the worst thing in the world. I had some light chores like gathering eggs or carrying in wood for the kitchen stove. But I was too little at that age to milk cows or do really heavy, nasty work like cleaning out the cow barn or hauling baled hay. And - I got to go to town a lot. By this time my older sister didn't want to go along much which was fine with me. Older sisters are pretty much a pain, and she was more interested in sitting in her room leafing through movie magazines and mooning over Tyrone Power.

Whenever the folks drove into town, they always went through the same ritual. Right after noon dinner, Dad would shave at the kitchen sink, and then dress up in his three-piece suit and tie. Mother would don a going-to-town dress, usually blue or black, along with a matching hat and a necklace rope of pearls. While shaving, Dad would ask me if I could spare the time to ride along. Goes without saying I usually could.

Mother always drove. She was a good driver while Dad wasn't. He liked owning tractors and cars but he didn't like driving them. When he was about forty-five, he gave up driving forever, thereby contributing to more restful nights for the sheriff's deputies and the motor-going public in general. As I said, Mother liked driving and traveling. Her oft-stated philosophy was, "if the car leaves the yard, I'm in it."

When we got to town, I went along with my folks to the bank - an imposing, formal kind of quiet place - almost like being in church except for lots of marble. Then with Mother to the dime store for needed supplies like sewing needles, thread, yards of cloth, buttons - boring things like that. Finally to the grocery store – loading up with sacks full of stuff like sugar, flour and cornflakes. While

paying the bill, Dad asked if I would like a small bag of salted pea-
nuts. Of course I did, and he handed the bag to me as we left the
store.

Driving home took about a half hour. I would ride in back,
usually crouched down on the floor. There, you could hear the rear
tires run over the cross-cut partitions on the pavement. Thwip -
Thwip - Thwip. I would imagine that a giant was following along
behind us, and each time his foot would hit the pavement after a
long stride, the sound his foot made would be Thwip.

Pretty soon I dug the bag of peanuts out of my pocket and
carefully, quietly, tore it open. They were delicious, peanut after
peanut after peanut. Thwip - Thwip - Thwip. Soon the bag was
empty. I silently folded up the cellophane bag and crammed it back
into my pocket. Just as I finished this little chore, Dad leaned over
the front seat and asked, in a pleasant tone, "How about breaking
open the peanuts?"

I was immediately faced with a problem. There was no bag
of peanuts to break open. So how to get out of this predicament.
Should I fib, and say that I had dropped the bag getting into the car?
That might be believed, and would have the added benefit of rain-
ing down sympathy on my head. "Poor little guy! Lost your bag of
peanuts! How brave of you not to cry. You should have told us. We
could have gotten you another bag."

I quickly rejected this ploy, both because it wasn't the truth,
and also because if it didn't work, I would be in double trouble as a
pig and a liar. What else? "The peanuts are no good. I tried one and
they're rotten." But if Dad asked to see the rotten peanuts, the game
would be up because there were no peanuts, rotten or otherwise, to
be examined.

"I already ate them," I admitted. (If it were done when tis
done, then 'twere well it were done quickly," as Macbeth eloquently
expressed it in another context). Put it right on the table, admit
guilt, take a little lecture on sharing and not being selfish, and then

move on. As I uttered the four fateful words, I tried to imagine some responses from Dad: 1) "Well, well - they must have tasted pretty good." (This accompanied by an amused, forgiving little chuckle.) 2) "Well, well, (no chuckle), I can't believe that you ate the whole bag without offering any to your mother and me."

Unfortunately, the second scenario is pretty much what actually took place. They were both a little shocked at my greediness, and I got the short lecture on sharing and generosity. After that the rest of the ride home was a silent one, except for the Thwip - Thwip - Thwip of the trailing giant. I suppose I did learn a lesson on sharing a bag of peanuts, although I don't recall, come to think of it, that Dad ever bought me another one. I like to think that my folks also learned a valuable lesson: never underestimate the greediness of a seven-year-old kid in the back seat of a car going home from town, with a little cellophane bag of salted peanuts clutched in his grubby little hands. Also - if you want a share of the peanuts, get your request in early.

LEFTY GOES FOR A KILLING

The other morning I ducked into the Beehive Café for my usual 8 a.m. breakfast. "Make a Beeline for the Beehive" is its so-called clever ad. It was the second of May already, and wouldn't you know, it was snowing, for crying out loud. Big wet globs of the stuff. Minnesota is the kind of place where it can snow just about any time, and probably has. Summer has nothing to do with it.

So I head for the counter and slide onto the stool next to my old pal, Lefty Sullivan. Went to school together, twelve years. Lefty is the sort who looks at you from the next stool like he's never seen you before in his entire life. No flicker of recognition. Gives me a two-second glance, then goes back to his American fries and undercooked eggs. Hardly even over-easy.

Lefty has always been called that because he was a left-handed pitcher in high school. He could bring it pretty good. Nasty curve, too, except it usually ended up in the dirt or behind the batter's head. Did I tell you he threw a no-hitter once? We were juniors and it was late April, cold and windy, really lousy baseball weather. Kind of day hitters hate because the bat stings your hands like hell, but Lefty loved it. Anyway, he hits the lead-off guy on the shoulder and didn't have much trouble after that. Most of them were afraid to dig in against Lefty. They had a helluva catcher, though, named Mike Lobesky. Funny how I remember him after all these years. In the eighth, he sent a screaming liner deep towards left center. I dove and just managed to snag it about three inches off the ground. Took some skin off my elbow in the process. When I got back to the bench, Lefty says, "So-so catch."

I forgot to tell you that Lefty's mom died just a couple weeks ago. Ninety-three years young as they like to say on those cheery talk shows. It was a nice funeral with a great lunch afterwards in the church basement. Ham sandwiches, two kinds of hot dishes, raspberry jello with sliced bananas in it, three kinds of cake, two chocolate, one white. Coffee.

"Too bad Ma can't be here," Lefty had said. "She'd love this."

Roxie, the waitress paused in front of me. She says things like, "I pause in front of the customer, breathlessly awaiting your order, sir." Smart-ass stuff like that.

"Number 3," Roxie said. "Wheat toast. Eggs over medium. Bacon not too crisp."

"Roxie," I said. "You're blessed with ESP."

"Oh," said Roxie, "that's nice. I'll probably get a big raise. Or a big tip."

I turned to Lefty. Miss your ma?"

"Yeah, I guess so."

"She's in a better place," I said.

"Better'n this, I hope," Lefty said, glancing out the window at the gloppy snow. Heavier now, you could hardly see across the street.

Roxie set my bacon, eggs, fries and toast in front of me.

"Need coffee?" she asked with a straight face.

"Does the Beehive need good customers?" I countered.

"Would that there were," Roxie said. Proving my point that a little grammar is a dangerous thing.

"So, what's up, Lefty," I asked. "And what are these two books I see in front of you. I don't recall you ever reading a book before in your entire life, specially in school."

"*Our Town*," says Lefty. "Thornton Wilder, the author. Same guy that wrote that bridge book."

"*Mr. Bridge?*" I ask innocently. "*Mrs. Bridge?*"

"No, no! A book about a bridge. *Bridge Over the River Tway*. You know, with that English guy in it."

I was getting lost. "In the movie, you mean?"

"Course in the movie," says Lefty with that beanball tone to his voice. "Pay attention."

Let me just say, parenthetically, that when Lefty uses a phrase like "that English guy," it could mean anyone from Alfred the Great to Sid Vicious.

"I think you mean *"The Bridge of San Luis Rey."*

"Yeah! That's it. 'Bout the bridge that snaps in Lima. Peru, not Ohio. Good story. Guy tries to figure out what makes God tick. Ain't too successful."

Suddenly I have a whole new respect for Lefty's hidden intellectual life. "So what's the other book," I ask.

Lefty picks it up, hands it to me. A little thin, battered-looking number that says *Baby's Record* in fancy angled lettering on the cover.

"A baby book," I say brightly.

Lefty forks the last cold bite of fried egg into his mouth. "These two books are gonna make me rich," he says with that tight little smile I've seen often.

"How so," I ask. Lefty is always in the process of becoming rich. Hasn't happened yet, though.

"Simple," says Lefty. "Look. At the end of Act 1 in *Our Town* - Lefty picks up the book, opens it at a marker - "Rebecca is talking to George. Ok? She's telling him about this letter that her friend - what's her name - here it is - Jane Crofut, gets from her minister. Following?"

"So far," I say.

"O.K., she was sick with something, this Jane gal, so her minister writes her a letter. Nice guy. And then Rebecca tells George how the letter was addressed. Still with me?"

"All the way," I say.

"O.K. The address says, 'Jane Crofut' (funny name) 'the Crofut farm, Grover's Corners, Sutton County, New Hampshire, United States of America." So then George asks, naturally, 'what's funny about that.' Then this Rebecca says, lessee, yeah, here it is: 'But listen, it's not finished: The United States of America; Continent of North America; Western Hemisphere; the Earth; the Solar System; the Universe; the Mind of God."

Lefty snaps the book shut and sets it gently on the counter as if he had just made some great point. "If you ask me," Lefty says, "nobody could get that much stuff on one envelope."

"All very interesting," I say politely, "but I don't see how -"

"Easy. Gimme the baby book. This here's my older brother's baby book that Ma kept. You remember he got killed in forty-four. Battle of the Bulge. Lookit. Here's his name. Lawrence Matthew Sullivan, born June 22, 1915."

"So?" I ask.

"So - what's interesting is what Ma wrote on the inside of the front page. Here. Read it yourself."

I look at the page. Written in a neat flowing hand was the following: 'Mrs. Sam Sullivan; Eyota, Minnesota, R.R. #1, Orion Township, Olmsted County, United States of America, Western Hemisphere, Earth, the Universe.

"Hey," I say, "that's really neat. What a coincidence."

"Ho, ho, ho," says Lefty, "coincidence, my Crofut."

"Well, what would you call it?"

Lefty leans towards me, both hands cradling his coffee cup. "Simple. Plagiarism. Look at the dates. *Our Town* came out in 1938. My brother's baby book in 1915."

I was beginning to see where Lefty was headed but thought it too wacky even for him.

"Look," says Lefty, "it's obvious. Somehow my ma and Thornton Wilder met somewhere, maybe at the Mayo Clinic, and they got to talking and visiting, and pretty soon she told him what she'd written in the baby book. He took it all down, changed it a little bit, and passed it off as his own."

"Lefty, that's the most cockeyed -"

"Only thing he added was 'the mind of God.' Funny Ma

didn't think of that. She was pretty religious."

"And you're pretty goofy in the head. But even in the one in ten billion chances you're right, how is that going to make you rich?"

Lefty smiled again, the one I knew all the way back to high school when he'd made up his mind to bean some skinny freshman shortstop.

"Simple. I file a lawsuit against Wilder's estate. Theft of intellectual property. Mental suffering. Pain and anguish. You name it. I figure I got a cut coming - what do they call it - a royalty - from every production of *Our Town* and every book sold from Day One. And wasn't there a move made of it, too, years back? Had that American guy in it. The actor. Same guy was in *The Bridge Over the River Tway*. Another coincidence, I suppose."

Lefty rubbed his hands together. "Yeah, I'll be so rich I'll buy this dump and turn it into a real café."

This last comment was directed at Roxie who was re-filling our coffee cups for about the fifth time.

Roxie snorted. "You and your riches. The time you get rich is the same time I'll get married again, which is never." This last line was delivered by Roxie as she waltzed into the kitchen.

"Well, good luck, Lefty," I said as I stood up. "By the way, what are you going to do if the lawsuit against Wilder goes nowhere?"

Lefty smiles that smile again. "Gonna look through all of Ma's stuff. She wrote a lot. Then I'm gonna see if any of it resembles anything of Hemingway. Or Steinbeck. Or Faulkner. Or what's his name. Fitzpatrick? Something like that. Used an initial for his first name. Lived around here once. Yeah." Lefty set his coffee cup down gently on the counter top. "That was back in the early twenties, wasn't it? He probably visited the Mayo Clinic, too."

I sighed. As I headed for the door, the snowstorm was in full swing. By now you couldn't even see across the street.

THE END OF THE WORLD CLIFFS

Tomorrow is my birthday. I will be fifteen years old. I like sitting here at the top of these cliffs that look out over the Root River Valley. It's warm here today with the sun sometimes shining, and sometimes hidden for ten or fifteen minutes by huge white clouds. The sun is shining now as I look out over the valley to the opposite side which is probably at least a mile away. I can only see part of the river because it's mostly hidden by trees. When the trees are fully leafed out in another couple of weeks, the river will almost entirely disappear.

The valley will be so beautiful then. A mass of green all the way across, and as far up and down the river as I can see. I will be fifteen years old tomorrow. I wonder if I will ever see sixteen. I know that I am destined to die young. I don't know what is happening to me. It's so strange and scary. I hear voices sometimes - inside my head. I talked to one of my friends a couple of weeks ago, Kathy, and asked her if she ever heard voices in her head. She just looked at me kind of weird-like, and said, no. She has avoided me since then. Am I not normal? Maybe I have been chosen by God for some great mission. But why should I be? Well, they say God works in mysterious ways.

I am standing here on the cliff. Daddy calls them The End of the World Cliffs because when he was little, his dad told him that the world ended here. It doesn't, of course. But if I stepped off the edge, my world would end very suddenly. I try to peer over the edge but my knees suddenly feel weak, and the ground slopes slightly downward. I crawl slowly on my stomach so I can look down. It must be a 100 foot straight drop, then a steep slope of rocks and bushes.

I try to picture myself (from outside myself) stepping off the

86

edge and falling through the air, turning over and over as I fall. Like in a movie I saw. Only in the movies, I think they use a stunt man or a dummy. This would be the real me. What would it be like to fall 100 feet like that, and then smash into the ground. When I was about ten, I fell off one of the beams in the barn and dropped about 15 feet into the alley way. It was covered with about a half-foot of chaff, so that I didn't get hurt much. But it happened so quick. One second I was running across the beam, and the next second I slammed into the floor. I guess I was dazed for a few seconds. Then I got up with nothing broken, just a few scratches.

But this would be different. If I fell a 100 feet, I would die. Well? Would that be so terrible? What would happen then? Would I go to Hell for killing myself? I don't know. I hope not. Sometimes I don't know if I believe in God or not. He is supposed to be loving. If he is, why does he make my life this hard? I feel so low a lot of the time. So "depressed." I heard that word awhile back and looked it up in the dictionary at school. And it's painful - this depression. I can feel it in the pit of my stomach, way deep inside. Sometimes Mom asks me if I'm sick, and I lie and say, no - I'm okay. I'm not sick in the usual way, you know, like throwing up, or having a sore throat or a headache or a temperature.

But something is wrong with me. I'm staring out over the valley and what I see is so beautiful. All the light green colors of early spring. There are some early wild flowers right here by my feet, pale blue with white centers. I know that if I pick them, they will die quickly. Die quickly. That has a nice sound to it. But flowers are just flowers, and I am a human being - a girl. I would die quickly if I stepped over the edge. The sun has come out from behind a large cloud. The light beats down on my face. It's so quiet here. No one here but me and the woods and The End Of The World Cliffs.

I have to start for home soon or Mom will get after me for being late gathering the eggs. If I die now, there won't be any more eggs to gather or floors to dust or dishes to dry or homework to do or school buses to ride or church to go to. I feel so lonely. I start to cry, and I had to stop writing for awhile because I couldn't see the page of my journal. The sun is still shining but I feel cold. I shiver. Oh! This is too hard to bear. Better to slide over the ledge and go down.

My folks will be sad for a while, I suppose. I wonder what it's like to have a child die. I have an older sister who lived only for a couple of days. We visited her grave last year. It's out in the country about a dozen miles away from the farm. A little, tiny country graveyard. What I remember most is that there are tall pine trees there, right among the graves. And this little grave marker, with her name on it and the dates of her birth and death. Only two days apart. Her name was Martha. She is my big sister but only lived two days. I wonder where she is now. Her body is in the ground and probably all gone by now. But her? Is Martha any where now? Does she still exist? Mom says that Martha is in heaven and sees God all the time and will be happy forever. I can't imagine what it would be like to be happy forever, or even happy for awhile. I wonder what God looks like or what people in heaven do all the time. I was thinking about my dead sister, Martha, this past winter, and I wrote a little poem about her.

> Tiny brief pilgrim
> Who lingered here
> Only a day,
> The spread wings
> And flew away.

I know that angels are different from us, but it's nice to think of her as a tiny angel with silver wings, flying up to heaven and being welcomed by God. "Well, Martha," He would say in a loud but kind voice, "you didn't stay on earth very long, did you. Well, you see, you are such a beautiful little thing that I couldn't bear not having you here with me."

I wonder what God would say if I killed myself. No angel wings for me, I guess. I would probably be carried up to the gates of heaven by a strong angel, still bleeding and crushed-looking. St. Peter would meet me at the gate and he would be frowning and serious-looking. "Well, what have we here," he would demand. "Some little girl who threw away God's gift of life. Some little girl who will never see her little sister who is with God."

Well, enough of that. I just scare myself thinking that way. What to do? I've got to decide in the next few minutes what to do. My palms are so sweaty I can hardly hold my pencil. I stare out over the valley. The air is soft and smells of spring. I decide that I will stand about 10 feet from the edge, close my eyes, and count to twenty-five. Then, keeping my eyes closed, I will walk straight ahead until I fall. I close my eyes and start to count one-two-three-four–seventeen–twenty–twenty-four, twenty-five. I stand still, not moving. It is so final. If I fall, there is no turning back. I can't fall 50 feet and then decide I made a mistake. I stand 10 feet from the edge of The End of The World Cliffs, my eyes shut, not moving. I scream at God that I don't love him, that he can keep his heaven, that I don't ever want to see him or Martha. Then I turn and stumble for home.

THE GREY FOX

I was about ten years old when I first visited a zoo. I had seen pictures or heard about most of the animals, and I had grown up with cows and horses, chickens and pigs, but this was different. You can get kicked by a horse or a cow, and a bull can be a mean customer sometimes, but for the most part, farm animals are a tame bunch.

The zoo was different. There you could see animals that were really dangerous: tigers, and lions, and bears. Not that I or the other people at the zoo that day were in any danger. But it was exciting to think that only steel bars or a glass wall separated you from some animal that would gladly tear you to bits.

I wanted to see the tigers first, as I figured they were about the most dangerous critters alive. I found them in a row of big cages that had thick glass fronts so you could see them perfectly. One especially caught my eye. He was the biggest of the lot, stretched out quietly, close to the glass. I remember I couldn't help shivering when he looked at me through half-closed eyes. He seemed bored and a little contemptuous of all the people staring in at him.

I went to see the monkeys next. They acted just as I thought they would, running about madly on the bars of their cages, and chattering incessantly. They were having a great time and seemed to expect laughter.

Next were the elephants. They looked as big as a barn to me and so heavy that I wondered if the ground could hold them up. The giraffes were so serious and kept dipping their heads a little as if they were afraid of banging against the sky.

So I wandered slowly about the zoo grounds, reluctant to leave one particular place and yet impatient to go on in order to see what was next. After a couple of hours, I came upon a small, rickety, out-of-the-way cage about ten feet long, and three feet high and wide with chicken wire sides. In it was a grey fox. I had never seen a fox before although there were a few around the farm where I lived. This fox acted differently from all the other animals I had seen in the zoo. Some of them had been sleeping, like the black panther; running and chattering and acting foolish like the monkeys; entertaining the people, like the bears in their huge grotto, who sat up on their hind legs and begged for food; fighting like the two bad-tempered lions who cuffed each other with sudden, hard blows; or peaceful, like the two beautiful, red and yellow birds sitting on the bough of the artificial tree with their heads close together. And all the other animals and birds had seemed contented in their cages, even though the tiger looked bored in his glass house.

The grey fox was none of these. He was not sleeping, didn't chatter; didn't clown like the bears, didn't look bored. He was doing only one thing with great intensity, tireless perseverance, and complete absorption. He was trying to escape. With head held down, he walked quickly back and forth across the length of the cage. When he came to the end, he wheeled about and paced quickly to the other end, and then back, and then back again. Back and forth, back and forth, quickly, silently. He didn't glance at me as I stood close to the chicken wire sides.

Every detail of that cage and its restless occupant is stamped on my memory, so that even now, many years later, I can see it perfectly in my mind's eye; I can see the chicken wire and dusty straw he walked on; the overturned pan in one corner, and smell the musty odor.

I thought then, as a small boy, that it was silly for the fox to act the way he did. After all, there was no possible way for him to escape; he couldn't bite through the wire or tear out the boards at the ends of the cage. He didn't even try to do these things. He just went back and forth, back and forth, quickly, tirelessly, endlessly. "Poor fox," I thought, "you will never get away." He just went back and forth, and my head went back and forth like a pendulum as I watched him, until I grew dizzy. How could he keep it up? Surely he must realize, even if he were only a stupid fox, that he was in a cage and that the door was closed and locked. That there was no escape. But the fox just went back and forth, back and forth.

"The only thing you will do is wear your feet off," I said aloud to him. "Things could be worse here, you know. What have you got to complain about? You get all you want to eat and a place to sleep. If you were out around the farm, you would have to hunt your food, and sleep in the rain sometimes, and it gets awfully cold in the winter. Besides, there's a bounty on you. You might get shot or trapped. How would you like to get your foot caught in a trap? Then you'd have something to yelp about."

After awhile, I was surprised to find that it was painful to look at him. I felt it was wrong, in some way, just to stand there and watch his agony. I didn't think of helping him escape which would have been easy enough. One end of the cage was a hinged door held shut only by a simple latch. One quick movement of my hand, and the fox would be out of the cage in a flash, under the wobbly snow fence that marked off the boundary of this corner of the zoo grounds, and across the fields into the distant October woods. There he would find soft piled leaves, wet underneath and brassy colored. Old fallen logs turning to powdery softness; gnarled grapevines, bare now of leaves, twisting up to the tops of oak trees, with a few bunches of small wild grapes still attached, bittersweet to the taste. There would be brambles and thorned, bare skeletons of blackberry bushes; stony, shallow creeks and rusty barbed wired remnants of old fences - hillsides and hollows, old lairs, trees beyond counting, and tall dry grass that could hide whole battalions of foxes. Open fields, some bare and dark now with Fall plowing, others with the stubbled remnants of this year's oats and the soft green promise of next season's alfalfa. Open sky and moonlight and first frosts and late at night the great hunter, Orion, striding up over the eastern horizon. And freedom. But I didn't think to open the cage.

I decided to leave. I walked away and then turned for one last look. The grey fox was striding back and forth, back and forth, quickly, tirelessly, endlessly.

DONNY

Growing up on the farm I knew a lot about dogs. We never bought one as most people do now because there were always dogs around. A dog would show up one morning, scared-looking and hungry. If you ignored him, chances are he would be gone by dark, looking for a welcome at some other place. But if you needed a dog, you would set out some food for the new arrival, and within a day or two, he would be settled in as if he had lived on the farm all his life.

That's how Shep became a member of our family. He showed up one day in early April, and since we didn't have a dog at the time, we invited him to stay. Shep was a good dog. He looked to be part Shepherd, about average size, black and white colored, and a good cow dog. Somebody had trained him well somewhere. His skill as a cow dog was important to me because it was my job in the sum- mertime to bring in the cows from the pasture about five-thirty each afternoon.

This could take a long time because our pasture was so big. Woods covered the far side of the pasture which ended in a deep valley through which a creek meandered. The milk cows liked to go down to the creek on hot summer afternoons. When I went to bring them in for milking, they would be clumped together by the creek, switching at flies with their tails, and looking stupid as only cows can. It was hard work getting them up the hill, and then it was a good half mile home to the barn. Now, with Shep, I could stay at the top of the hill and send him down to bring them up.

Some dogs will try to run cows too fast, and some can't control them at all. Cows will chase after a timid dog, and gener- ally act sassy. If that happens, you're better off leaving the dog at home. Shep drove the cows just right. He didn't rush them along too fast, but he didn't let them dawdle either. He had a way of letting the cows know who was in charge by an occasional nip to their heels, and they didn't challenge his authority. A cow dog also needs courage because even the most agile dog can get kicked sometimes. When that happened to Shep, he would come right back and nip the culprit on the heel again. He was a good cow dog.

I was eight years old when Shep came along. Everybody in the family liked him, but he became my special friend, maybe because I was the youngest. Dogs seem to like little kids best. And we worked together since I was the official cow-fetcher.

We also went for walks in the woods. The neighboring farm had a big pasture that ran along the north side of our yard. This pasture had a lot of woods in it, too. It was fun to go on walks there and Shep always came along. Sometimes, just for fun, I would try to sneak away without him but he always knew what I was up to. Within a couple of minutes, he would come pelting along, barking up a storm. He would snuffle along the trail, sprint off in one direction, suddenly change course, disappear for a minute or two and then dash out from the thick clump of underbrush, tail wagging, his coat matted with burrs. If he treed a squirrel, the racket made by the yelping dog and the scolding squirrel was almost unbearable. Shep would leap as high as he could, unconcerned that his prey was sitting on a branch 30 feet off the ground. When I finally got him to quit this nonsense, he would charge off on a new trail.

Once in a while I tried to teach Shep to fetch sticks, but with no success at all. Shep was not a retriever, and wasn't about to learn. I would throw a stick as far as I could, and yell out "fetch!" Shep would stay sitting on the ground, peering at me intently, his head bent to one side as if saying, "too bad about your stick, but there's nothing I can do about it."

I remember the first winter Shep was with us, mostly because of the skunk. Ella and I came home from school one frigid afternoon, and as usual, Shep bounded across the neighbor's pasture to meet us. When we got to the house, no one was home. Our folks had gone into town, and Donny and Ray weren't back from high school yet. We fixed ourselves a snack and warmed up in the kitchen. It felt good inside after the cold walk. Ella went up to her room to change and suddenly, I heard her scream. She came tearing down the stairs yelling, "my gosh, Shep's got a skunk over in the pasture!"

We pulled on our coats and overshoes as fast as we could and ran outside. Sure enough, there was Shep in the pasture, just across the back yard fence. Facing him was a skunk that was trying to get around Shep so that it could head down the hill into the woods. Shep would have none of that. What he wanted to do was to kill that skunk except that he couldn't get close enough to do it. While Ella and I watched, freezing our hands because we had left our mittens in the house, Shep charged the skunk, fangs bared. When he got within a dozen feet or so, the skunk reared up on his front legs and blasted Shep with his scent. Shep yowled, retreated, and rubbed his head in the snow to try and wash off the awful stink. In the meantime, the skunk tried to edge its way closer to the hill, but then Shep charged again with the same result. It was like he was on a chain. He could get so close to the skunk, and no closer. This kept up for a good half hour. Both Ella and I were getting hysterical by this time because Shep refused to give up, although we tried over and over to call him off. I guess we were afraid he was going to die of rabies or a heart attack.

Finally, Donny and Ray drove into the yard in the pick-up. Donny was a senior in high school, Ray only a sophomore. Donny got the rifle out of the kitchen, and during one of Shep's retreats, killed the skunk with one shot. The smell was just awful. I had never been that close to a skunk before, dead or alive, and that was the closest I ever wanted to get again. Since skunk pelts were worth several dollars, Donny skinned it. I couldn't watch even at a distance and I thought Ella was going to be sick. Ray sneered at me for being a sissy, but I didn't care. That night, Mother banished Shep to the barn. He usually slept on top of the cellar door next to our front porch. He had an old blanket to snuggle under, and would sleep there on all but the coldest of winter nights. But not for the next week.

Two days after the skunk incident, Pearl Harbor was attacked. We soon became involved in projects like saving scrap iron and old rubber. I remember we ended up with a huge pile of scrap metal - rusty fence posts, broken wheels off of machinery, even old fence wire - and a big truck hauled all the stuff away one day. Soon we were getting ration stamps for gasoline and sugar. I was fascinated by airplanes and tried hard to memorize the silhouettes of all the enemy fighters and bombers, although it was unlikely that German or Japanese planes would ever get as far as Minnesota. I fell in love with B25's and P40's and worried about enemy submarines.

The next summer, Donny went into the Army. He was a good baseball player in high school, captain of the team as a senior. He was also the only really good hitter on the team. They didn't win a single game that year, and Donny got a little discouraged by it. That same year, he batted .600. He hit six lead-off triples that season but died on third base every time because nobody else on the team could hardly hit a lick. I kept telling him that he should hit home runs instead. He would laugh a little and then chuck me on the side of the head. I tried to copy his batting stance, but it wasn't easy because Donny batted right-handed while I was a lefty.

He used to play catch with me all the time during the summer. Dad and Ella and Ray and Donny and I would play softball almost every afternoon for an hour. When Donny pitched, he always tossed the ball easy so I got a lot of hits. Shep enjoyed the game, too. When I ran to first base, he would tear along beside of me, beating me to the bag. Dad would yell, "Shep's safe, Joe's out." He thought that was pretty funny, I guess.

At any rate, Donny went into the Army in June of 1942. We all missed him, and it was a lot more work for everybody on the farm. Dad used to say during that summer that he had never realized how much work Donny did, and what a good farmer he was. It was also a hot, rainy summer. Because of the heat, the cows stayed down at the creek almost every afternoon. They were usually in a bad humor because of the heat and the flies.

On July 4, Shep got kicked hard in the head by one of the cows. He yelped in pain and tumbled backwards. After a few seconds, he seemed okay, a little dazed but he kept behind me as I drove the cows into the barn. That night he hardly ate anything at all. Dad looked at the swelling on Shep's head and said he thought Shep would be fine in a day or two.

But he wasn't. Within a week, we realized that Shep couldn't see very well any more, and that he was shaky on his feet. He would stand up and then almost fall back on his haunches. He started running into things. By the middle of July, he wouldn't go with me any more to help get the cows. I remember one afternoon especially. I whistled for Shep to come as I started out for the pasture. He got up from his perch on top of the cellar door and trotted slowly behind me, head down. About halfway across the pasture, he suddenly turned in a wide half-circle, heading back for the house. "You come back here, Shep," I yelled. He only ran away faster. "Damn stupid dog," I screamed at him. I was upset mostly because the cows were nowhere in sight, it was hot, and I felt as put upon and worked to death as a 10-year-old can get. "Why aint Donny here?" I whined as I headed into the woods. I knew where those stupid cows were. Clear down at the creek, as far as away from the stupid barn as stupid cows could get. Mother noticed that night that I was moody and asked what was the matter. "Nothing," I lied.

From that time on, Shep wouldn't respond at all when I called him to help with the cows. I complained to anyone who would listen that Shep was not pulling his weight, that he was lazy and stupid, and that we should get rid of him and get a dog that wasn't afraid of cows. Dad asked me how we should get rid of Shep. I didn't know.

"He doesn't feel good," Dad said. "I think we should wait awhile to see if he gets better. Meantime, Ray will get the cows every other day." Ray wasn't very happy about that. He said he was too grown up to do kid's chores.

By the time school started in September, nothing had changed as far as Shep was concerned. He wouldn't help with the cows or anything. It was like not having a dog at all. I went for walks in the woods alone, and when Ella and I came home from school at the end of the first day, no Shep came running to meet us. He just lay on the cellar door, not eating much, not even barking any more when a strange car drove into the yard. I could tell that the folks were worried about Shep but they kept putting off doing anything about him. I still felt mad at Shep, but I guess I was starting to realize that he probably was sick, not just acting ornery.

In the middle of October, Donny came home on furlough. We were all tremendously glad to see him and he couldn't seem to get enough of Mother's biscuits. He also looked different. It wasn't just the uniform. He looked like a man, not just my big brother any more. He said I looked different too. "Gee, you've grown a couple inches, Joe." He punched my arm.

Two days before Donny was due to go back to camp, he met Ella and me as we were coming home from school. He said he wanted to talk to me. Ella, looking a little miffed as only big sisters can, went on home. Donny and I walked along the cow trail that wound its way down the hillside and into the woods. It was a beautiful October afternoon, the kind of weather that makes winter seem a long ways off.

I could see that Donny had something to tell me and that he was having a hard time getting to it. "Is it about Shep?" "Yeah. It's about Shep. Dad and I have been talking and we've kind of decided that Shep has to go." "Go where?" I asked densely. I suddenly felt protective about Shep even though I had done nothing but complain about him for the past few months. "You know," Donny said.

He sat on an old log and dug at the ground with a stick. The afternoon sun slanted in warmly. There was no breeze at all, and a gold haze filled everything. Death seemed far away. "You know," Donny repeated. "Shep hasn't been himself for quite awhile now. Every since he was kicked this summer. He might go crazy all of the sudden and attack somebody. Ella or you or Mother."

I stared at Donny. I knew now what "has to go" meant. "I'm sorry," Donny said. "I also need your help. Shep won't let me come near him at all. We've got to get him away from the house so I can use the rifle." I looked at the ground. "What I want you to do - Joe, are you listening?" I looked up in the general direction of Donny. "What I want you to do is see if you can get Shep to follow you out to the cattle shed. I'll wait in the shed." "When? I couldn't get the rest of it out. "Right now," Donny said. "What!" I yelled. "It's not going to be any easier tomorrow, is it?" I didn't say anything. "Okay," Donny said. "Now listen. He hasn't been fed anything yet today. You have to try and get him out to the shed with some food. I'm sorry, but Mother insists that we have to get him away from the house." "What if he won't go with me?" "I don't know!" Donny sounded angry. "We'll have to try something else then. But let's try this first. Okay?"

I didn't say anything. I stood up. We started back toward the buildings. I kept thinking that Shep would be dead in a half hour. He was alive now, but he would be dead in just a little while. I started to cry. Donny put his arm around my shoulders as we walked along. "I'm sorry," he said. "Life can be really tough sometimes." "Yeah," I said.

When we got to the house, Donny lifted the rifle off its hook and put a box of shells in his jacket pocket. He said, "give me five minutes to circle out to the shed." He nodded to the folks and went out the side door, away from the front of the house where Shep slept. I looked out the front window. Shep was lying on his old blanket in his usual spot, on top of the cellar door. Tomorrow we would bring in a load of firewood. The chunks for the furnace and the sticks for the kitchen stove would be thrown helter-skelter down into the cellar until they overflowed up to the sidewalk and against the side of the house. Ella and I would then dig out the stove wood, toss it over the partition and stack it in cords against the opposite wall. Shep would not be around to see any of this or run alongside the wagon as we headed out to the woods.

I poured some milk into Shep's pan and dropped two thick bread crusts into it. It was Shep's favorite supper. As I went out the front door, I met Ray coming in. He had seen Donny heading out towards the cattle shed with the rifle. "Finally gonna get rid of that stupid dog, eh?" "Shut up," I said.

I walked up to Shep. His eyes were closed. I hoped he was dead but it didn't seem likely. "Hey, Shep." The fake heartiness in my voice almost made me sick. "That's right, boy. Keep your eyes open. Are you hungry? Come on, fella. That's a good dog. Let's go for a walk, Shep. No, you don't have to help with the cows. Come on, you need the exercise. Yeah. You've been lying around so long, your bones are gonna get stiff. Come on, we'll walk across the yard. Come on, boy. You're doing fine. Here Shep, I'll open the gate for you. You used to be able to jump over this with no trouble at all when we went to get the cows. Remember that? We'll go over by the shed, and then you can eat. Here's the straw pile. Remember when we were threshing last summer? That was fun, wasn't it. All those wagons to chase after. Remember all the noise? And the dust! Boy, I'm glad threshing only comes once a year. Here's the shed just ahead. Let's just walk around to the front, and then you can eat. Good-bye, Shep."

As we rounded the corner, Shep saw Donny with the rifle. He growled and started to circle away from the shed, back towards the house. I stared at him as he swerved unsteadily, and then the rifle cracked beside me. Shep howled as the bullet plowed through his left hind leg. I heard Donny mutter, "damn," heard the rifle bolt slide back, the empty shell plop softly to the ground, a fresh bullet inserted, the bolt slide forward. By now, Shep was a good 150 feet away, dragging himself through the dust of the barnyard. His leg looked broken, and I could see the blood. Donny ran towards Shep, the rifle half raised. I yelled, "damn you, Donny."

I wanted Shep to die, to be out of his misery. I couldn't move. I watched Donny come up close behind Shep, to within 10 or 15 feet. My folks were standing by the windmill, just on the other side of the fence. Ray and Ella were beside them. Shep stopped. By now he had drifted away from the general direction of the house and was facing out towards the pasture. He turned his head back to lick his wounded leg, and saw Donny. He bared his fangs. I saw Donny raise the rifle, hold it motionless. Shep started to turn and the rifle cracked again, its echo rolling into the distance. Shep lay on the ground, still.

I ran out of the barnyard towards the pasture. I heard Donny yelling for me to come back, heard Dad yelling. I kept going, down into the woods. When Donny left for camp two days later, I went into the woods again. I hadn't spoken to him since he killed Shep. On the day he left, Dad was going to drive him into town about two in the afternoon to catch the train. I snuck out of the house a little before noon, and didn't come back until dark, the October night raw and windy. My folks were pretty mad at me, of course. I didn't know where Shep was. Donny had buried him over in the neighbor's pasture. I didn't want to know where.

Donny was killed the next spring in North Africa. On April 8, 1943. They sent his things home. He had been driving an ammunition truck that blew up. I'll never forget Mother's face when the news came. She went deathly white and sat down. After a few minutes, she started to cry, just staring straight ahead, the tears running down her face with Ella trying to comfort her. Dad cried, too. I found him the next day in the barn, sitting on a milk stool, his face in his hands, sobbing. He kept saying, "my poor little boy. My poor little boy." Ray was standing behind him, his arm around Dad's shoulders. Ray kept saying, "it's okay, Dad. It's okay." He was crying too. They didn't see me. Ella cried for about a week, it seemed. I remember she couldn't go to school for awhile. She wouldn't eat, and the folks were afraid she was going to be really sick.

Fourteen days after the telegram, we got a letter from Donny. It had been mailed the day before he was killed. The rural mailman, Mr. Butters, drove into the yard to find Dad. He wanted to soften the shock as much as possible. The folks always said afterwards that had been real thoughtful of him. The last part of Donny's letter was for me. He hoped I wasn't still mad at him. He knew how much I loved Shep. He had loved Shep, too. It was just that there was nothing else to do. He said I should study hard in school and help Dad and Ray out as much as I could. He hoped he could come home soon, but it looked like the war might go on for a long time yet. He said he loved me.

I started to cry. It was awful because my throat hurt so much I could hardly breathe. I finally went out of the house and across the yard to the barnyard gate. Tip trotted beside me. He was a big, skinny dog that had showed up one morning about three weeks earlier, half-starved and mangy-looking. He wasn't much good as a cow dog, but he did his best. I climbed over the gate, and Tip tried to jump over it. He got almost halfway over, then scratched wildly as he felt himself sliding backwards. He backed off from the gate and made a couple of false starts before his nerve deserted him completely. I finally opened the gate for him.

We walked past the straw pile which was almost all gone now, around the cattle shed and across the pasture towards the woods. Tip crashed along ahead of me, making enough noise to scare off anything within a mile, hot on the scent of a rabbit or something. After a minute, he came bounding back, tail wagging, slobbering. "Donny will never come back," I thought. I sat down on a damp log and dug at the ground with a stick. I stared at the still bare trees. "I love Donny," I said to Tip.

EXPIATION

In his *Life of Johnson*, James Boswell records the conversation Johnson had with a young clergyman in which Johnson stated that "he could not in general accuse himself of having been an undutiful son." But on one occasion in his boyhood, Johnson admits that he refused to go with his father to Uttoxeter-market, not far from his native town of Litchfield, England. Johnson tells the clergyman that the remembrance of that disobedience was "painful." "A few years ago," Johnson continues, "I desired to atone for this fault; I went to Uttoxeter in very bad weather and stood for a considerable time bareheaded in the rain, on the spot where my father's stall used to stand. In contrition, I stood, and I hoped the penance was expiatory."

One day when I was about thirteen, I got into it with my dad. He wasn't the easiest man to work for, and at my age then, you tend to draw some lines in the sand. It didn't hurt that I was a very big kid having gone through a recent growth spurt.

That late spring morning, I was driving the horses, harnessed to the hay wagon, up alongside the granary to load some grain sacks onto the wagon. My two older brothers and my dad were waiting inside the building. To make a long story short, I didn't get the wagon close enough. Dad got very nettled and yelled at me to drive around again and get the damn wagon closer.

I exploded, I think I can say without exaggerating too much. I shouted, and yelled - "I can never do anything right! Every damn thing I do is wrong! I ain't putting up with this crap one minute longer," and much more of the same. I don't remember all of the exact words, but you get the general idea.

I don't think my dad had ever been sassed that way before by any of us kids. He looked a little shocked and said something to the effect that his two sisters, my aunts, were visiting from California and he didn't want them hearing language like that.

I hadn't run out of gas yet, though, and I screamed that I didn't give a damn if they heard it or not, and more along that line. This happened a long time ago, and I don't remember much of what else went on that day. I know I drove the wagon around again and got it closer to the granary. I know my two older brothers never said a word about it to me then or ever. My dad never mentioned the incident again. Neither did I. It's the only time I've ever raged like that and it didn't leave me with a good feeling. This, by the way, is the first time I've talked about the incident to anyone. It's safer now. My dad, my mother, and the two aunts from California have long since passed away. My two older brothers who never said a word are both dead. All the witnesses gone, you see. And life goes on as it always does.

One day I left home for college. Dad eventually sold the farm to my oldest brother, and moved to town with my mother. In his later years, when I came to visit, his eyes would light up and he would say something like, "Well, it's Tommy boy! How are you?" And I would go over to his chair and kiss him on the cheek.

Right now, I'm probably about the same age, give or take a few years, as Samuel Johnson was when he stood bareheaded in the rain at his father's old stall at Uttoxeter. I've been standing here for a "considerable time," myself, and a light rain is falling. It's early September, and the country cemetery is a lovely place, still very green, the ground sloping down gradually to the highway that runs along one side. Beyond the road stretch out huge fields of corn readying for harvest in a few weeks.

I wonder if I've stood here long enough. I think of Samuel Johnson. Had he asked a passerby whether he had atoned sufficiently, the stranger might well have said, "Oh, certainly. Your father understands. Don't you think he loved you, Samuel? Don't you realize that he was a flawed man, too?"

At some point, Johnson packed it in and went home, his shoes wet, the danger of pneumonia always a threat in his time. I will go home now, too. I haven't prayed any here. But then Johnson didn't either, as far as we know. I haven't said to my dad, "Sorry about that in the past. Sorry I blew my top."

I head for my car, parked on the gravel road that bisects the graveyard. Dusk is coming on. Misty rain yet. It is very still. The dead never say a word. At least not out loud.

A Few Trifles

THE GOOSE SOLUTION

Several years ago, a goose problem developed out around the airport. Geese were ignoring the no-fly zone, and generally making a nuisance of themselves. The solution was to corral a goodly number of the offending birds and ship them off to Oklahoma (somewhat akin to disposing nuclear waste in Nevada, since what we don't like we tend to shift somewhere else. Let them deal with it for a change). The hope, probably in vain, was that the geese wouldn't come back, although they could easily have beaten the truck back to Minnesota. The report I wrote on this incident got mislaid somewhere – which seems to happen often lately – and it was only by chance that I happened upon it recently. So here it is, somewhat dusty and dated.

They're gone by now, the geese, trucked all the way to the Choctaw Indian Reservation in faraway Oklahoma, where the wind comes sweeping – but you know the rest.

Partly from curiosity, and partly out of the sense of civic duty, I hurried out to the Carlos Avery Wildlife Management Area in Anoka County to interview the geese before their forced departure. As I neared the 280 milling-about birds, one of the biggest of them, wearing a sleeveless fleece jacket and John Deere cap sideways on his head, waddled toward me. "Honkers the name," he hissed, "Fred. You a reporter?" "Well," I stammered, "not really. But I do write letters to the editor sometimes." "Good enough," said Fred. "Now listen carefully and get this out to the public." "Aren't you guys a hazard to the public?" I interrupted. "Hanging out by the airport, being a threat to Northwest Airlines? Ah – excuse me – Delta Airlines?" "Hogwash," Fred snapped. "We were just looking over the place." "For what?" I asked. "For next year, dummy. For when we take over." "Take over?" I asked numbly. "Take over the airport? You can't do that. It's federal property or something."

"Course, we can," said Fred. "Perfect landing spot for us geese. You read the papers? How they tried to wipe us out? Well, there's too many of us now. Just a few hundred in the area thirty years ago, and now? Thousands and thousands. Check out Silver Lake in Rochester." Fred's eyes narrowed. "And that's just a start what with global warming." "But taking over?" I asked quickly as the geese were starting to be herded toward the semi for their trek south. "Didn't I tell ya?" Fred cackled. "Next year tens of thousands of us. Take over the airport, and then expand outwards to Burnsville, Bloomington, Richfield, Edina." He smacked his lips. "Downtown Minneapolis, the Mall, then east, following 94. St. Paul. The east side. Golf courses – those greens are delicious."

Fred was shouting as the geese disappeared into the truck. "Little Canada, Newport, 3M." Fred was gone now, all the geese inside the truck, the doors slammed, the engine roared to life, the truck began moving slowly. I ran alongside just as Fred muscled his way to the side of the truck and poked his head out through the slats.

"Know what the Indian authorities in Oklahoma said when they heard you guys were coming?" I yelled as the truck picked up speed. "They said 'yum, yum! And pate, too.'" Fred sneered. "No problem. We'll be back." He screeched as the truck started to pull away. "No stopping us now. Nobody's safe from us. Nobody! West St. Paul, Fridley. White Bear Lake – all that water." And the last word I heard him scream out as the truck rounded a corner and vanished from sight was, "Woodbury!"

MRS. ZENO PUTS HER FOOT DOWN
(or at least tries to)

There's this fellow, Zeno, an ancient Greek, who had some really strange ideas - one being that change is not possible, and what we think of as change is just illusion. I know - I know - sounds wacky, but for instance, he said that you couldn't ever cross a room because (stay with me on this) to reach the opposite wall, you have to get halfway across - get it? Okay - but before you get halfway across, you have to get halfway to halfway, and so on and so forth. And since you can keep dividing space into halves forever, at least theoretically, you can never cross the room, because you don't have forever to do it. Something like that. Can't even get out of your chair. Sort of an early Greek version of a couch potato.

I suppose it's okay to think this way as long as you don't try to pull such stuff on your missus. Which, I've learned recently from some newly discovered ancient documents I'm not at liberty to divulge.

What happened was this - Mrs. Zeno asked her hubby to take out the garbage - a perfectly reasonable request. But old Zeno tried to weasel his way out of this chore (something most husbands can relate to), by claiming that it wouldn't be possible to reach the trash bin because he would first have to get halfway there, you see, and before that, halfway to halfway, etc., etc.

How did Mrs. Zeno react to this shabby excuse? Not too kindly, I'm afraid. She said something like, "Look, Mr. Know-It-All, Smarty-Pants philosopher, either the garbage goes out now, or, I'm coming over there - watch me cross the whole room - and stomp down on your foot."

Zeno was now caught, not in a philosophical but in a real quandary. It's one thing to deny the possibility of change in theory

- and quite another to face the verbal wrath and physical assault of a size ten sandal crashing down on your corns. Ms. Zeno stopped in front of her seated, cowering spouse. She raised her right foot a good 18 inches in the air. "Watch my foot," she rasped. "Watch it descend not just half way onto your footsie, but ALL THE WAY!"

Unfortunately, my ancient sources stop here abruptly, practically in mid-sentence, like Thucydides's History of the Peloponnesian War. But I think it's safe to assume that Zeno came to his senses in time to jump up and do as she who must be obeyed, commanded. At least that's what I would have done in the same circumstances. After all, it's one thing to state that Achilles will never catch the tortoise because of the head start the turtle has but don't try telling that to an odds-maker at the track. And don't try to outface Mrs. Z when she gets that tone in her voice and that look in her eye.

THE JACK AND JILL CAPER

Jack and Jill
Went up the hill
To fetch a pail of water
Jack fell down
And broke his crown
And Jill came tumbling after.

Let us begin by considering Jack and Jill themselves. Note that only their first names are given. Significant? Perhaps. Certainly makes identification difficult.

It's usually assumed that Jack and Jill are brother and sister, and also young – children in fact. But does this interpretation stand up to serious scrutiny? But first, a few other observations.

1. Why did Jack and Jill (whatever their relationship and age) go *up* the hill. Why not *down* the hill. Now, you may reply that the well, assuming a well was their destination, was up the hill from their starting place. Which brings up another interesting point. Why are we not informed about this so-called "starting place." Was it a farm house? A cottage? A cabin? Why all the secrecy? How are we to get to the bottom of this business without clear and unambiguous evidence!

2. Putting that aside for a moment, let's consider what I call "The Problem of the Pail." We are told precious little about this crucial object. Was it a wooden pail? A tin pail? A plastic pail? And how large was this mysterious pail? A gallon? Two gallons? Assuming for the moment that Jack and Jill really are children, and young ones at

that, the pail could hardly have been over two gallons at the most.

3. But this aside, we come upon the most puzzling aspect of the pail mystery, namely, what happens to it subsequently. Why does the pail seemingly vanish? We see Jack and Jill tumbling down the hill. Why not the pail as well? There is something slightly sinister about this suddenly invisible pail. Did it somehow trip up Jack and Jill and then skedaddle in order to avoid answering embarrassing questions from the authorities?

4. Now we must deal with the most serious matter of all, for which I have already hinted at as a possible answer. Why did Jack and Jill fall down so precipitously? They don't just trip and fall on their faces. No. They tumble down which implies a long, rolling fall. And not only that. The fall is so severe that Jack actually breaks his crown, that is, strikes his head, possibly against a stone during this disastrous accident. And I use the term "accident" guardedly, because whether this really was an accident or a deliberately planned criminal action is still to be resolved. May never be solved in fact.

5. Putting that aside for a moment, we have to inquire again, why did Jack and Jill fall? Young children are agile and quick footed. And surely this was not their first trip to fetch water. They would have been well aware of any potential danger. But notice that we are given no indication what time of year this tragedy took place. Had there been an ice storm the previous night? But surely, responsible parents would not have sent their children out on such a dangerous mission.

Which brings us to my interpretation of what really happened. Jack and Jill were not children at all but a middle-aged married couple. For a long time now, Jill had tired of Jack and the monotonous life on their little hard-scrabble farm. After falling in love with the local miller named Joe, Jill had persuaded Jack to take out a million dollar double indemnity life insurance policy.

On the fatal day, Jill persuaded Jack who was suffering from a hangover, to go up the hill with her to "fetch a pail of water," as she expressed it. On the way down she tripped Jack, who suffered a fatal crown breaking, then collected her two million dollars, and ran off to the Bahamas with Joe, the miller. The authorities never suspected a thing, which is somewhat surprising because while Jack "broke his crown," Jill suffered only superficial bruises. The pail, by the way, was never recovered, hardly surprising considering the fact that Jill and Joe have been observed numerous times cavorting on the beach using a little plastic shovel to fill a two-gallon tin pail with sand.

THE CANDLESTICK EMGMA

Let us turn our attention to one of the briefest and most enigmatic of the Nursery Rhymes, namely:

> Jack be nimble
> Jack be quick
> Jack jump over
> The candlestick

Certainly, the salient feature of this trifle is its brevity – a mere eleven words. As if the author took to heart the dictum that less is more, here indeed, to an almost absurdist degree. Nevertheless, there are clues aplenty lurking within these four lines that should allow us to get to the core of the matter in order to wrench out, so to speak, the real meaning.

So – we begin with Jack. That name again – the same as in Jack and Jill. Surely a clue not to be overlooked. Is this indeed the same Jack, only this time alone. Why is Jill excluded? Is candlestick jumping (a rather inane practice if observed closely) thought by the author to be an unsuitable activity for a girl? And what are we to make of the fact that Jack's name is repeated as the initial word of the first three lines. Does the author suppose that our power of memory is so feeble that we won't remember Jack's name unless it is constantly reiterated – thrown into our faces, as it were.

Leaving that aside for the moment, we must now consider the significance of candlestick jumping. And in connection with that, an interesting phenomenon emerges – the narrator. In *Jack and Jill*, the narrator is just that, someone who simply tells us what happened, much like in a newspaper account. But – in *Jack be Nimble*, quite a different situation obtains. Here, the narrator does not so much relate what happens, rather – he (or she) commands the attention in the imperative voice – "Jack, you will be nimble – no ifs, ands, or buts. Jack – you will be quick (if you know what's good for you). Jack – you will jump over the candlestick, even if a lighted candle is placed on top, even if you have to practice weeks on end to do it."

And who is this ordering voice? A parent? A coach? Is Jack training for an Olympic Candlestick event? Is Jill hiding in the background, anxious and afraid for her brother's welfare, but too terrified to voice her concerns?

And Jack himself. What does he think of this whole situation? Is he a good athlete to begin with? Or does he fail, time after time, to clear the hated candlestick. Does he feel like Sisyphus, condemned to forever push his rock up a hill, only to have it come tumbling down again, like Jack and Jill in their infamous quest "to fetch a pail of water." Is Jack not really nimble or quick at all? Why else should he be ordered, commanded, harried to be those things which he is not.

Perhaps there are no answers to these questions. Sadly we must leave Jack, and as we depart the scene, our last glimpse shows us a darkened room, lit only by a feeble candle, stuck atop a candlestick which Jack, bravely but futilely tries again and again to overleap.

THE HUMPTY DUMPTY DISASTER

Humpty Dumpty sat on a wall
Humpty Dumpty had a great fall
All the king's horses and all the king's men
Couldn't put Humpty Dumpty together again

In seeking to unravel and penetrate to the core of this mystery let us, for the sake of brevity, refer to Humpty Dumpty simply as H-D.

It would be almost impossible to name any other fable or nursery rhyme that presents more difficulties or ambiguities than the four lines that make up the H-D story. Perhaps the best way to approach the problem is to examine each line and even each word in each line to see what results so that clarification can be apprehended.

First line: H-D sat on a wall. What a myriad of mysteries reside in these few words. Who is H-D? Why is he sitting on the wall? How high up is his perch? What material is the wall constructed of? Brick or stone or wood? What is beyond the wall – that is, for what purpose does the wall exist? The only thing we can be sure of is that H-D is sitting on top of the wall. But why is he there? Is he a guard of some sort? A spy? Is a football team holding a secret practice on a field behind the wall?

And who exactly is H-D. He is usually pictured as a large egg with arms and legs, wearing a hat, shirt and tie; a kind of dandy. But the poem itself is silent as to the essence of H-D. Could he not be a rabbit or a chicken (that is, a hatched out egg)?

Second line: Humpty Dumpty had a great fall. Here the story suddenly takes a sinister turn, but notice how coy the author is.

H-D had a great fall. First, let us grasp the obvious. It was a high wall. This was no low garden wall, across whose wide top a child might romp with no fear of injury should she lose her balance and topple to the ground. This was a great fall. Might we estimate it at thirty, forty, or even fifty feet?

If H-D actually was an "egg," such a fall would have resulted in a disaster, especially if the landing spot was hard ground or a stone sidewalk. In real life, if someone suffers such a fall, 911 is immediately dialed, and First Responders rush to the scene. What actually occurs in the nursery rhyme? Just about the most ridiculous and unbelievable response imaginable.

Let us repeat the third and fourth lines:

> All the king's horses and all the king's men
> Couldn't put Humpty Dumpty together again.

So here we have poor H-D, lying seriously injured, probably expiring on the spot. And what is the response? A whole troupe of soldiers on horseback come crashing onto the scene, not only demolishing any evidence, but also H-D in the process, probably not leaving enough of him to make up a decent fried egg sandwich.

And so, sadly, because of this wanton destruction of evidence, we shall never ascertain what H-D's mission was, (what he was after) and whether or not more sinister forces were at work – that is, did he fall accidentally, or was he pushed? Tragic accident – or murder?

Definitions

Plagiarism – extinct now, fortunately. In medieval times, an ailment that afflicted authors, for some peculiar reason. Symptoms were fever, itchy fingers, shortness of breath, and acute counterfeitism. The last recorded case was an obscure late 17th century French amanuensis who claimed to be the real author of Bacon's version of Shakespeare.

Unabridged – what happens to the countryside as the result of floods or bombing and strafing raids. They are good places to avoid on moonless nights.

Mawkish – one who actually likes war. The origin of this term is somewhat uncertain, but the most generally accepted theory is that it derives from a now extinct bird, akin to the kestrel. Just why the mawkish died out is still a subject for speculation. An interesting sidelight is that the last mawkish was observed in 1186 A.D., the time of the Third Peasant's Revolt.

Canonize – to reduce a fortress to rubble by banging away at it with big guns. It was soon discovered after the invention of artillery that this was a much more efficient method than shooting arrows or even slings of outrageous fortune.

Oxymoron – a somewhat dated form of insult that originated at Oxford University in the 13th century. As a term of opprobrium, it was used by rich young lords against poor country lads who were trying to work their way through college by washing pots and pans in the refectory. Use of the term rose to a climax in 1298, then vanished abruptly after the Fourth Peasant's Revolt of 1299.

Egalitarianism – the theory that we are equal because we all come ultimately from the same egg. (Also known as the Big Egg Theory). There are metaphysical difficulties involved here, of course, especially if you try to explain this theory to the biggest rooster in the barnyard. It also poses serious problems in regard to the "which came first, chicken or egg" controversy, which most scholars agree, is far from settled, although that is about the extent of their agreement.

Tenet – a device you put up for a weekend out in the woods somewhere. It always rains about six inches on such occasions. Tenets become so uncomfortable then, that they are sometimes exchanged for a motel room.

Non Sequitur – referring to inane expressions like "have a nice day" which are usually said to you as you arrive at the office on a rainy morning, late, because your car wouldn't start.

Platitude – a flat, elevated area not much good for anything. The wind blows there a lot.

Soliloquy – a speech delivered by an actor alone on stage because another actor has missed an entrance, and is still down in the green room finishing a cigarette.

Kismet – what usually doesn't happen at the end of the first date, at least in old Doris Day movies.

Free Will – a slogan scrawled on walls in London when Shakespeare was imprisoned briefly in 1596 for non-payment of a debt.

Onomatopoeia – the last word asked in a spelling contest.

Defense Mechanism – what a football coach, whose team has absorbed a 47-0 shellacking, tries to work out before next Saturday's Homecoming game.

Genus – someone who is really smart, like Einstein. Not everyone can be a genus, of course. Most of us have to settle for being a specious.

Inspiration – what happens to you if you are unlucky enough to be walking by a church with a tall, sharp-pointed steeple that suddenly gets knocked down by a strong wind.

Blank verse – what a poet who is experiencing a dry spell, ends up with after staring at the computer for two solid hours.

Deus ex machina – a curse uttered by Roman charioteers when the axle would break near the end of a race in the Circus Maximus.

Dehydrated – a really washed-out feeling experienced by Dr. Jekyll after a bad night out.

Postseason – the time of year when a lot of coaches get fired.

Spoils system – the result of not cleaning out the back of the refrigerator at least once every three months.

Malpractice – what a football team has evidently been having all week when it gets clobbered 49-0 on a Saturday Homecoming afternoon.

CPSIA information can be obtained
at www.ICGtesting.com
Printed in the USA
FFOW01n2055250614
6012FF